National curriculum mock test
Key stage 2

Mathematics

Paper 3: Reasoning

Each test takes 40 minutes to complete.
Each test contains 20 or 21 questions, with
35 marks available in each test.

MOCK TEST A

MOCK TEST B

MOCK TEST C

MOCK TEST D

MOCK TEST E

© SatsPapers.org.uk. These tests are not associated with the Standards & Testing Agency.

SATS PAPERS 2016 ONWARDS

SATs results levels are **scaled scores**. A score of 100 represents the "national standard" and the raw mark in which it directly reflects is calculated once all the SATs papers have been marked. This allows test results to be reported consistently from year to year. If two children achieve the same scaled score on two different tests (despite possibly having achieved different "raw scores"), they will have reached the same attainment. Level 6 papers have been scrapped and the standard papers have more challenging questions to stretch the most able children. The lowest scaled mark available is 80 and the highest is 120. A raw score of 2 or less is not scaled and no score is provided.

The interpretation of scaled scores is as follows:

Score	Interpretation	Scaled Range	Raw Scores
< 100	Below Expected Standard	80-99	3% to 54.5%
100	At Expected Standard	100	54.5% to 58%
> 100	Above Expected Standard	101-120	58% to 100%

Maths Content (use www.CoolCleverKids.co.uk for preparation)

Paper 1 40 marks (arithmetic) includes

- Fractions (including mixed numbers).
- Decimals (including converting fractions into decimals).
- Percentages (and how they relate to fractions).
- Square numbers.
- Rounding numbers.
- Applying Addition, subtraction, multiplication (long and short) and division (long and short) coupled with order of operations *(BODMAS/BIDMAS)*.

Paper 3 and Paper 3 (Reasoning) carry 35 marks each both span 40 minutes and are based upon more problem-solving and includes knowledge of paper 1 concepts and include:

- Geometry (including coordinates, rotation, reflection, symmetry etc).
- Ratios and proportions (and how to interpret them from fractions, percentages etc).
- Charts and tables.
- Units and measures (including time, money, temperature, weight, volume etc).
- Shapes and their properties (including triangles, hexagons and their angles).
- Roman numerals.
- Statistics (Mean, mode and median).

These papers are similar to the previous non-calculator Paper A and calculator Paper B (except with problems that do not require the use of a calculator).

CoolCleverKids.co.uk

Because it's Cool to be Clever ™

Although SATs papers changed in 2016, in reality Paper 1 (mental maths) has been replaced with arithmetic and Papers 2 and 3 are similar to previous papers 1 and 2, except calculators may not be used. CoolCleverKids has over 13 years of SATs style papers that can be undertaken online. Even most calculator papers can be undertaken without a calculator, bar 1-2 questions and stretches the most able children.

Why waste time marking SATs papers yourself?

Using CoolCleverKids.co.uk children can undertake tests online, have tests marked instantly and are provided with explanations. They can even save partially completed tests and return to them later. Correction or ad-hoc tests can be created. Children can enrol on to courses with tasks appearing in a child's dashboard.

A full history of tests is stored with responses so they can be revisited or discussed. Performance reports indicate strong and weak areas.

The system contains lesson notes, worksheets, links to video presentations and tests with a comprehensive times tables application. Numerous SATs style papers and 11+ tests have been uploaded together with audio for mental maths. Subscribers enjoy unlimited access together with explanations for test questions.

CoolCleverKids has been used for years with children gaining exceptional SATs scores and grammar school success with minimal parental involvement.

As a bonus, KS2 SATs English spelling and science tests are available to undertake online. For those preparing for 11+ exams, NVR questions are also included.

The maths programme aims to make maths easier for children. It focuses on the basics of maths, from first principles, ensuring a solid foundation and then building upon basic concepts via lessons notes, video-clip examples worksheets together with comprehensive tests.

Tests enable a child to practice and Sats style tests can be undertaken online in a test or exam mode, which are automatically marked. The unique programme goes one step further and provides explanations to accompany answers enabling a child to understand how questions should be answered.

The primary school maths programme encourages self-study, self-discipline and concentration, all attributes that are vital later on in life.

A demo of CoolCleverKids is available at: www.CoolCleverKids.co.uk by clicking DEMO.

Instructions For All Tests A-E

You **may not** use a calculator to answer any question in this test.

Questions and answers

You have **40 minutes** to complete this test.

Follow the instructions for each question.

Work as quickly and as carefully as you can.

If you need to do working out, you can use the space around the question.

Some questions have a method box like this:

Show your method	

For these questions you may get a mark for showing your method.

If you cannot do one of the questions, **go on to the next one**.
You can come back to it later, if you have time.

If you finish before the end, **go back and check your work.**

Marks

The number under each line at the side of the page tells you the maximum number of marks for each question.

National curriculum mock test

Key stage 2

Mathematics

Paper 3: Reasoning

You have 40 minutes to complete this test which contains 20 questions, with 35 marks available.

First name	
Middle name	
Last name	
Date of birth	**Day** **Month** **Year**
School name	

MOCK TEST A

1 Here is a diagram for sorting numbers

Write **one number** in each box.

One is done for you

	Multiple of 9	**not** a multiple of 9
Multiple of 4		**16**
Not a multiple of 4		

2 marks

2 Here is part of a number line

Write the missing numbers in the boxes.

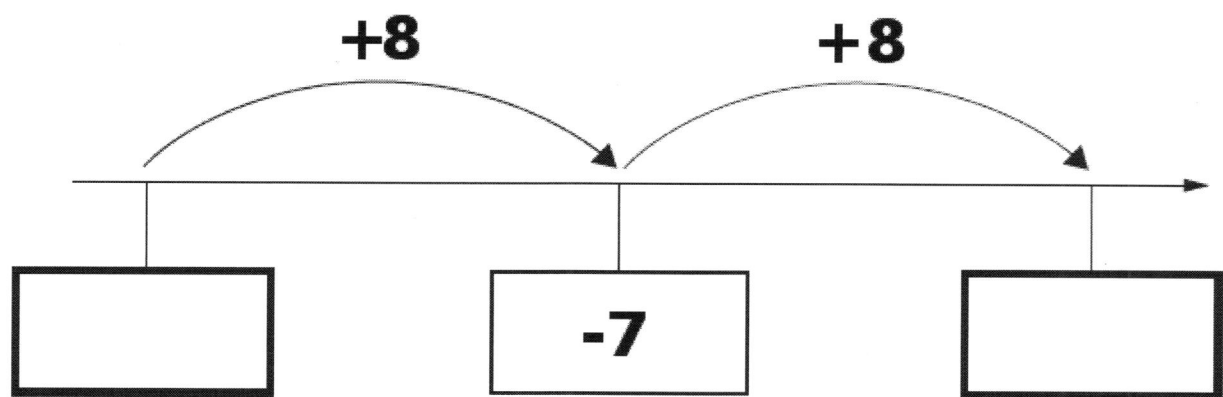

2 marks

3 Look at his number

32,785.79

Write the **digit** that is in the hundreds place

☐

1 mark

Write the digit that is in the hundredths place

☐

1 mark

4 A sports club plans to collect £300 between June and October. The chart shows how much they collected by the end of September.

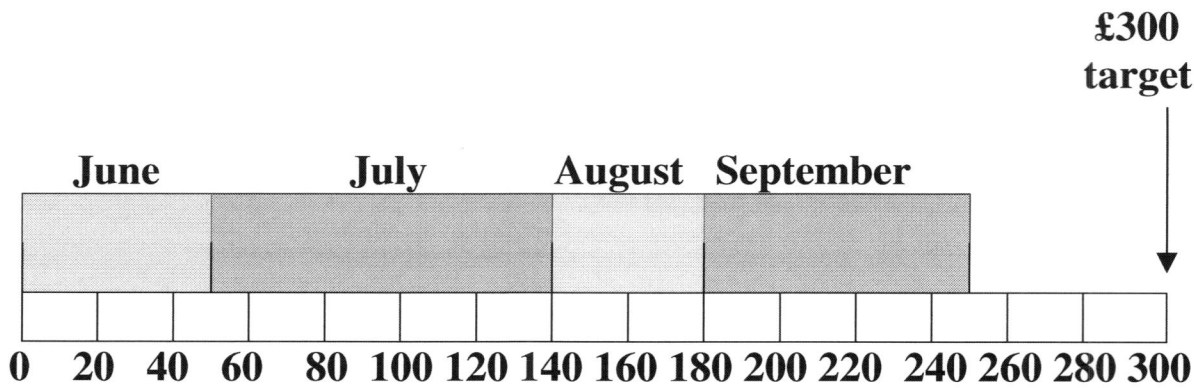

Write the name of each month where they collected more than **£65**

_____

1 mark

How much money did they collect in July and August **altogether?**

£ [   ]

1 mark

5 Chung pours 65ml of water in to a cylinder.

Draw an arrow on the cylinder to show the level of the water.

1 mark

6 Here are six cards

| × 1000 | × 100 | × 10 |
| ÷ 1000 | ÷ 100 | ÷ 10 |

Use a card to complete each calculation.

7.6 ☐ = 0.076

7.6 ☐ = 7600

7.6 ☐ = 0.76

2 marks

7 Write the number 67,983 in **words.**

1 mark

8 Here is a shaded shape on a grid.

The shape is translated so A moves to B

Draw the shape in its new position.

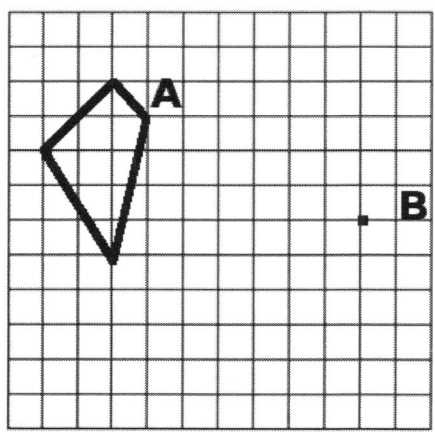

Use a ruler

2 marks

9 The mass of a 2p coin is 7.2g.

The mass of a 1p coin is half the mass of a 2p coin.

What is the mass of these six coins altogether?

Show your method

g

2 marks

10 A pack of four sweet tubes costs 80p.

A pack of six chocolate bars cost £1.50.

How much **more** one chocolate bar cost than one sweet tube?

Show your method

[   ] p

2 marks

11 Write the four missing digits to make the **addition** correct.

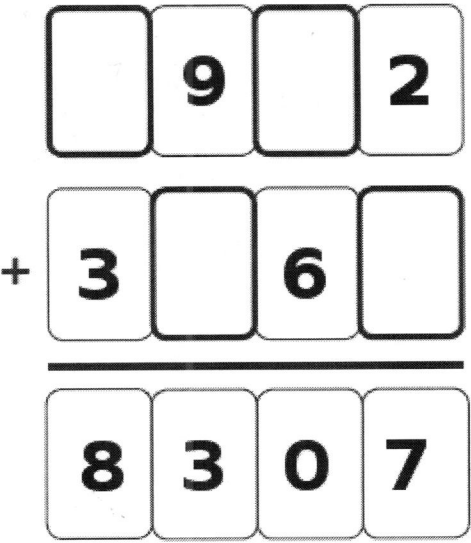

2 marks

12 Two decimal numbers add together to equal 1.

One of the numbers is 0.006.

What is the other number?

1 mark

13 There are four fraction cards

$\frac{4}{6}$ $\frac{5}{8}$ $\frac{6}{12}$ $\frac{7}{18}$

Use any three of the cards to make this correct.

☐ < ☐ < ☐

1 mark

14 Here is a number pyramid.

The number in a box is the **product** of the two numbers below it.

Write the three numbers.

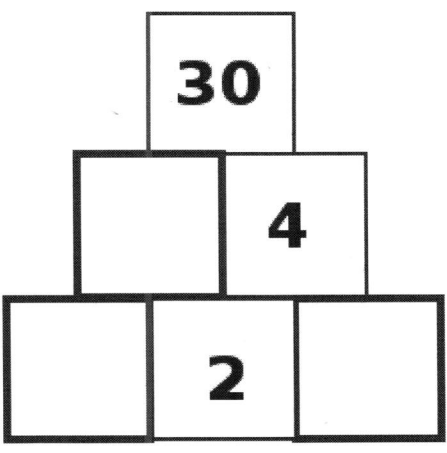

2 marks

15 Join dots in the grid to make a quadrilateral with **1 obtuse** angle.

1 mark

16 Lisa chooses a number less than 200.

She divides the number by 4 and then adds 13.

She then divides her number by 2.

Her answer is 12.5

What was the number she started with?

Show your method

2 marks

17 This shape is made of 20 equally sized rectangles.

What **percentage** of the shape is white?

%

1 mark

18 Here are the ingredients for a cake.

Baking spread	240g
Self-raising flour	220g
Caster Sugar	100g
Brown Sugar	80g
Eggs	4

Sam has only 60g of brown sugar to make the cake.

How much baking spread must he use?

Show your method

[ ] g

2 marks

19 The area of a tennis court is 196 square metres.

A squash court measures 9.8 metres long by 6.4 metres wide.

How much larger is the area of the tennis court than the area of the squash court?

Show your method

[ ] m²

3 marks

20 Here are two identical shaded triangles on coordinate axes.

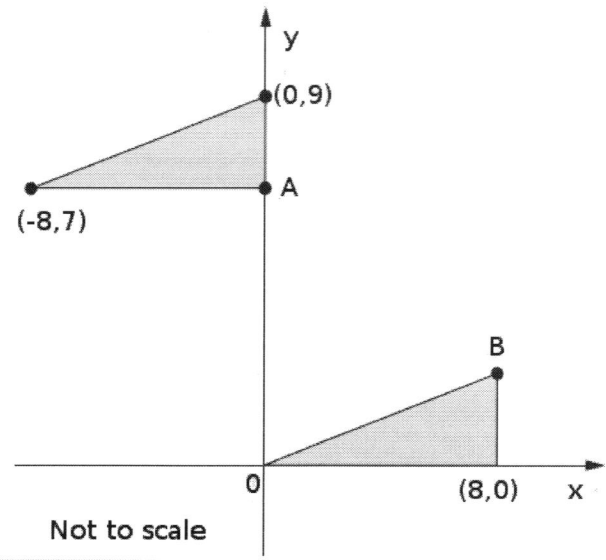

Not to scale

Write the coordinates of points A and B

A = (,)

B = (,)

2 marks

The test is now over. If you have time, check your answers.

National curriculum mock test

Key stage 2

Mathematics

Paper 3: Reasoning

You have 40 minutes to complete this test which contains 21 questions, with 35 marks available.

First name	
Middle name	
Last name	
Date of birth	**Day** **Month** **Year**
School name	

MOCK TEST B

1 The numbers in this sequence increase by 16 each time.

Write the missing numbers.

☐ 78 94 ☐ 126 142 ☐

2 marks

2 This table shows the temperature at 8am during three days in October.

15th October	18th October	25th October
+7 °C	-5 °C	+2 °C

What is the difference between the temperature on the 15th October and 18th October.

 °C

1 mark

On the 30th October the temperature was 5 degrees lower than on the 25th October.

What was the temperature 30th October?

 °C

1 mark

3 A clock shows this time twice a day.

Tick the **two** digital clocks that show this time.

| 03:15 | 04:15 | 14:15 | 16:15 | 18:15 |

1 mark

4 Each shape stands for a number

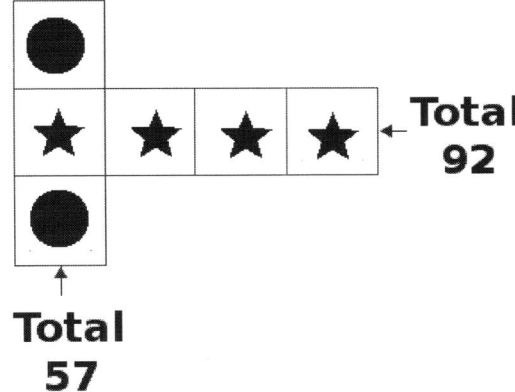

Work out the **value** of each shape.

★ = ☐ 1 mark

● = ☐ 1 mark

5 Write these numbers in order starting with the **smallest.**

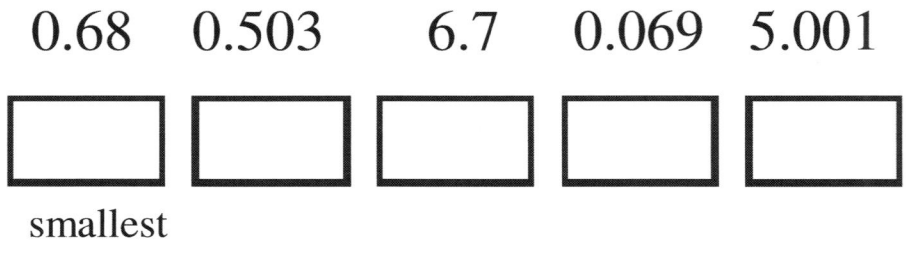

0.68   0.503   6.7   0.069   5.001

☐ ☐ ☐ ☐ ☐
smallest

1 mark

6 John cuts 5 metres (m) of string in to **four** pieces.

The length of the first piece is **2** metres.

The length of the second piece is **1. 27** metres.

The length of the third piece is **1.32** metres.

What is the length of the fourth piece in cm?

Show your method

☐ cm

2 marks

20

7 Here are five angles marked on a grid of squares.

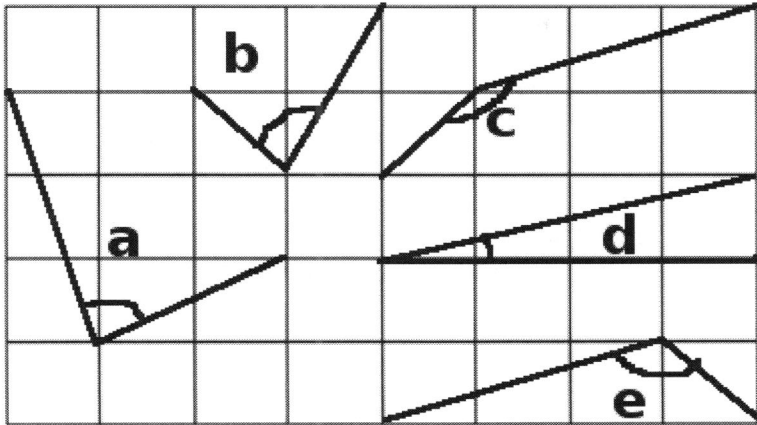

Write the letters of the angles that are **acute.**

[   ]

1 mark

Write the letters of the angles that are **obtuse.**

[   ]

1 mark

8 Olive buys four pencils.
She pays with a £2 coin
This is her change.

What is the cost of one pencil?

Show your method

p

2 marks

9 Here is part of a train timetable from Coventry to Birmingham New Street.

Coventry	7:55	8:23	8:48	9:01
Canley	7:49	8:28	8:56	9:05
Tile Hill	7:54	8:32	9:02	9:10
Birmingham International	8:04	8:43	9:13	9:19
Birmingham New Street	8:19	8:59	9:30	9:39

How many minutes does it take for the 8:56 from Canley to reach Birmingham International?

[   ] minutes

1 mark

Mr Egar is at Tile Hill at 7:55.

What is the earliest time he can reach Birmingham New Street?

[:   ]

1 mark

10 Elle makes a cuboid using 12 cubes.

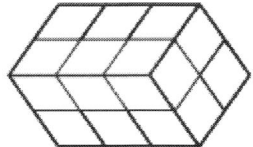

Write the letter of the cuboid that has a different volume from Elle's cuboid.

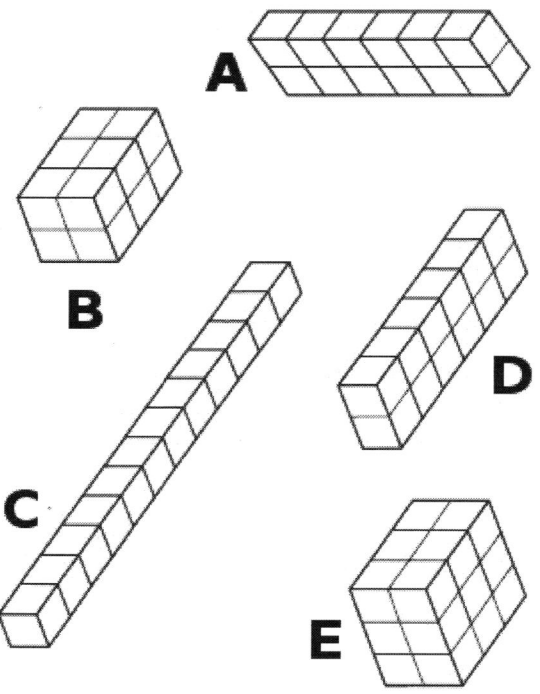

_____

1 mark

11 A shop orders 12 boxes of biscuits.

Each box contains 8 packs of biscuits.

Each pack contains 28 biscuits.

How many **biscuits** did the shop order?

Show your method

2 marks

12 A triangle is translated from position **A** to **B**.

Complete the sentence

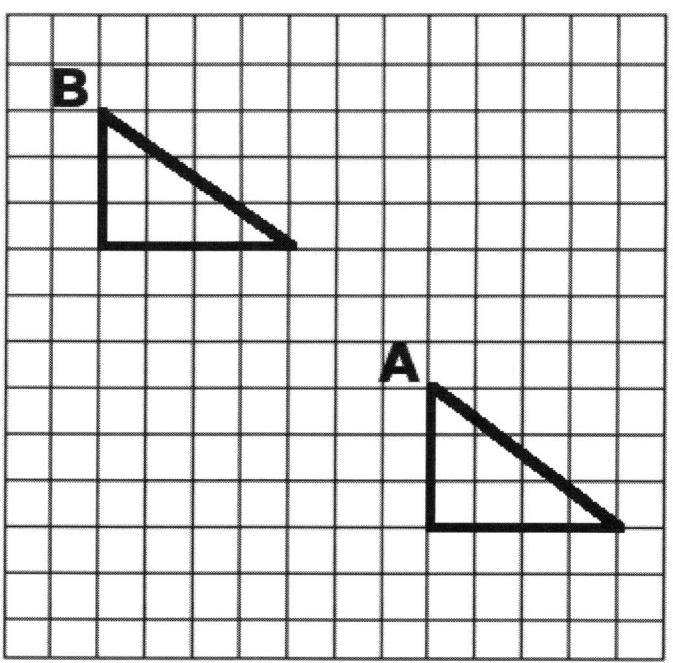

The triangle has moved ☐ squares up

and ☐ squares to the left.

1 mark

13 Lisa chooses a number.

She divides it by 3 and then subtracts 7.

She multiplies this result by 4.

Her answer is 28

What was the number she started with?

Show your method

2 marks

14 Complete each sentence using a number **from the list below.**

$$120 \quad 168 \quad 1{,}176 \quad 4{,}032 \quad 10{,}080$$

There are ⬜ hours in a week

1 mark

There are ⬜ minutes in a week

1 mark

15 Complete this table by rounding the numbers to the **nearest hundred.**

	Rounded to the **nearest hundred**
30,635	
3,063.5	
306.35	

2 marks

16 6 stars have the same mass 7 circles.

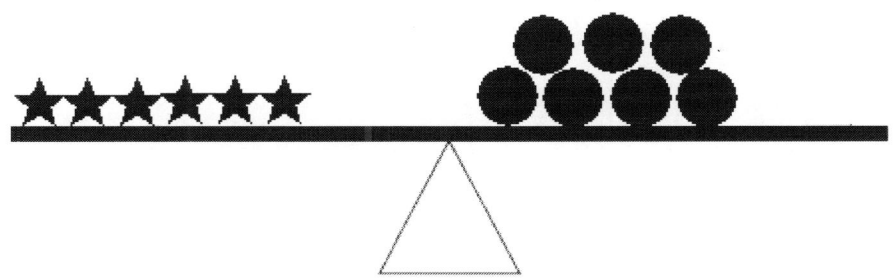

The mass of a star is 3.5g

What is the mass of a circle?

Show your method

☐ g

2 marks

17 Here are five triangles on a square grid.

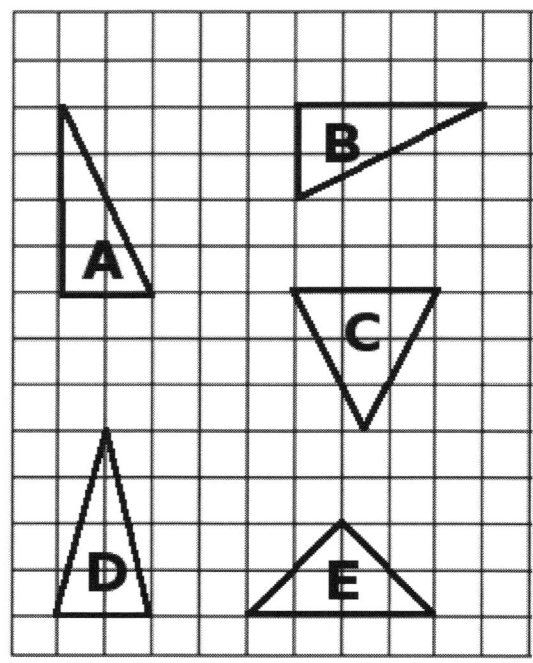

Four of the triangles have the same area.

Which triangle has a **different** area?

1 mark

18 The diagonals of this quadrilateral cross at right angles.

Tick **all** quadrilaterals that have diagonals which cross at right angles.

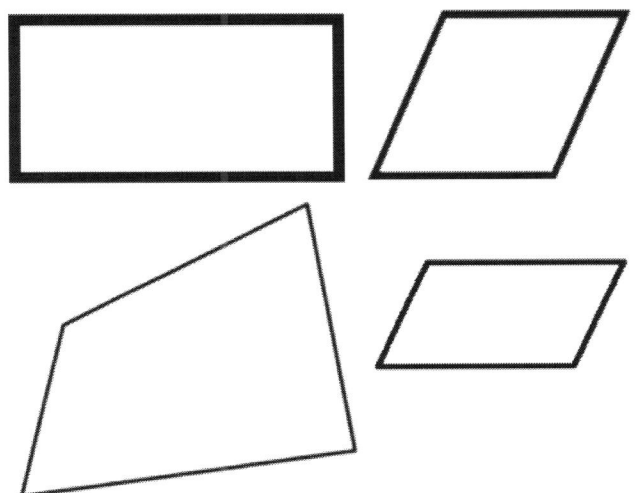

1 mark

19 Circle the two numbers that multiply to equal 1 million.

250   1,000   4,000   10,000   500,000

1 mark

20

Lisa had some money.

She spent £1.50 on some soup.

She spent £0.75 on some rolls.

She had one-quarter of her money left.

How much money did Lisa have to start with?

£ .

2 marks

21 6023 ÷ 317 = 19

Use the above fact to find the answer of
18 x 317

2 marks

The test is now over. If you have time, check your answers.

National curriculum mock test

Key stage 2

Mathematics

Paper 3: Reasoning

You have 40 minutes to complete this test which contains 21 questions, with 35 marks available.

First name	
Middle name	
Last name	
Date of birth	**Day** **Month** **Year**
School name	

MOCK TEST C

1 Here is a diagram for sorting numbers.

Write **one number** in each box.

One is done for you

	Multiple of 3	**not** a multiple of 3
Multiple of 7		
Not a multiple of 7	**18**	

2 marks

2 Write the missing numbers in the boxes.

$7 \times 11 = \boxed{}$

1 mark

$\boxed{} \times 12 = 84$

1 mark

3 Look at his number.

61,427.31

Write the **digit** that is in the **thousands place.**

[ ]

1 mark

Write the **digit** that is in the **tenths place.**

[ ]

1 mark

4 The local scouts were raising funds for a trip overseas. The chart shows how much they collected by the end of August.

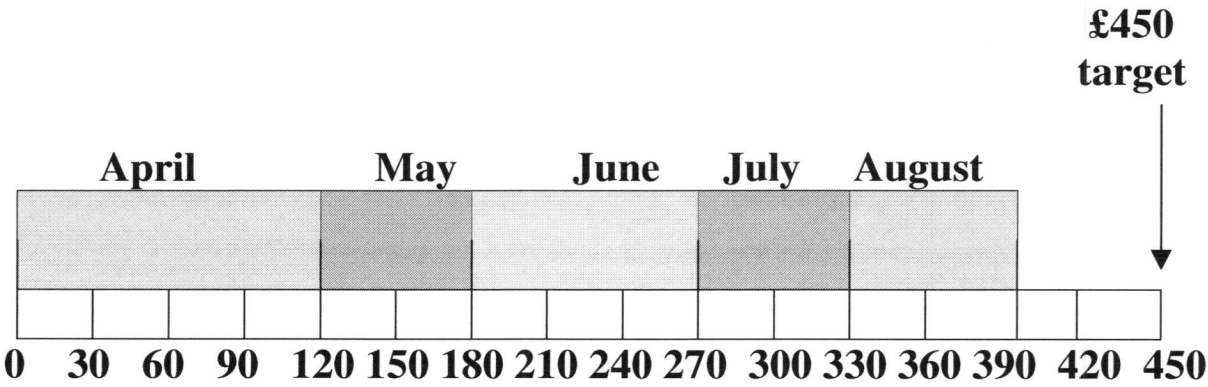

Write the name of each month where they collected the same amount of money.

_____

1 mark

How much money did they collect in April and June **altogether**?

£ ☐

1 mark

5 The cylinder contains water and the level is shown by the horizontal line.

Tim pours 65ml of water out of the cylinder.

How much water was left in the cylinder?

[ ] **ml**

1 mark

6 Here are six cards

| × 1000 | × 100 | × 10 |
| ÷ 1000 | ÷ 100 | ÷ 10 |

Use a card to complete each calculation.

1.01 [ ] = **101**

10.01 [ ] = **0.01001**

0.101 [ ] = **0.0101**

2 marks

37

7 Write the number 66,724 in **words.**

_____

1 mark

8 Here is a shaded shape on a grid.

The shape is translated so A moves to B.

Draw the shape in its new position.

Use a ruler

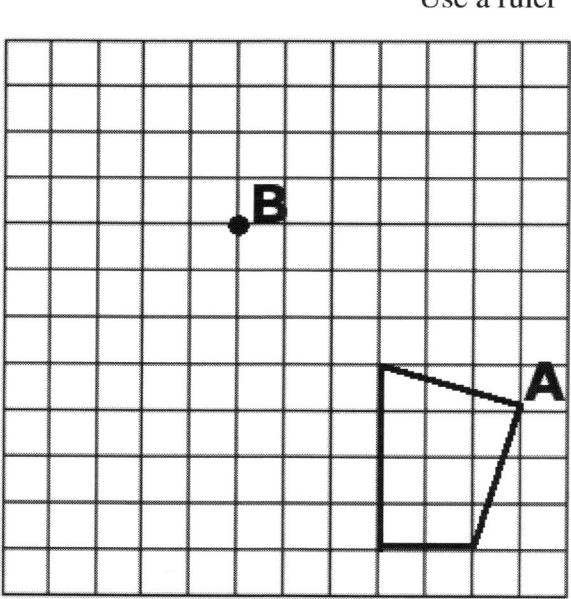

2 marks

9 The mass of a 5p coin is 3g.

The mass of a 10p coin is twice the mass of a 5p coin.

What are the mass of these six coins altogether?

Show your method

g

2 marks

10 A pack of four tubes of tennis balls costs £2.80.

A pack of two tennis balls and a rule book costs £1.75

How much does a **rule book** cost?

Show your method

£ .

2 marks

11 Write the four missing digits to make the **subtraction** correct.

```
   9 7 0 1
 - 2 5 8 6
 ---------
   7 1 1 5
```

2 marks

40

12 Two decimal numbers add together to equal 1.

One of the numbers is 0.043.

What is the other number?

1 mark

13 There are four fraction cards.

0.51   0.47   0.50   0.4

Use any three of the cards to make this correct.

☐ > ☐ > ☐

1 mark

14 Here is a number pyramid.

The number in a box is the **product** of the two numbers below it.

Write the three numbers.

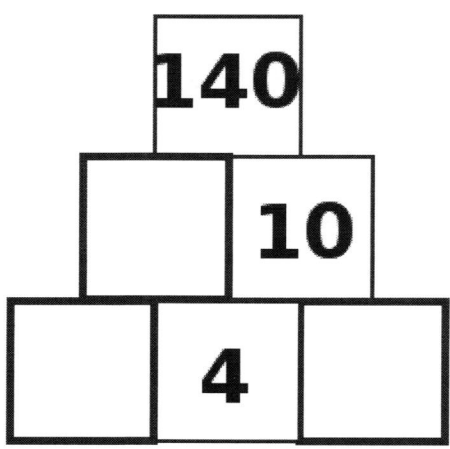

2 marks

15 Join dots in the grid to make a quadrilateral with **2 obtuse** angles.

1 mark

16 Lee chooses a number less than 100.

She divides the number by 3 and then adds 12.

She then divides her number by 4.

Her answer is 8.5

What was the number she started with?

Show your method

2 marks

17 This design is made of 20 rectangles.

What **percentage** of the rectangles is grey?

%

1 mark

18 Here are the ingredients for a cake.

Double cream	400ml
White caster sugar	100g
Eggs	5
Whole milk	125ml
Unsalted butter	25g

Sam has only 25ml of whole milk to make the cake.

How much white caster sugar must he use?

Show your method

[ ] g

2 marks

19 The area of a badminton court is 82 square metres.

A volleyball court measures 18 metres long by 9 metres wide.

How much larger is the area of the volley ball court than the area of the badminton court?

Show your method

m^2

2 marks

20 78 x 79 = 6162

Use the above fact to find $\dfrac{6162 + 1}{79}$

1 mark

21 Here are two identical shaded triangles on coordinate axes.

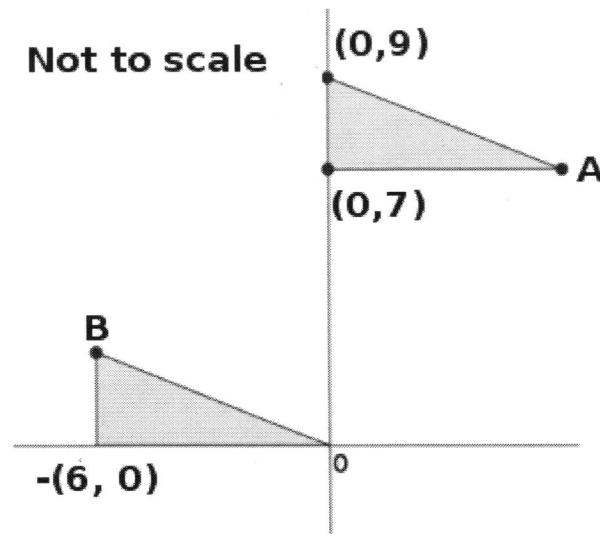

Write the coordinates of points A and B

A = (,)

B = (,)

2 marks

The test is now over. If you have time, check your answers.

National curriculum mock test

Key stage 2

Mathematics

Paper 3: Reasoning

You have 40 minutes to complete this test which contains 20 questions, with 35 marks available.

First name	
Middle name	
Last name	
Date of birth	**Day** **Month** **Year**
School name	

MOCK TEST D

1 The numbers in this sequence increase by 18 each time.

Write the missing numbers.

| | 68 | 86 | | | 140 | 158 |

2 marks

2 This table shows the rainfall on three days during April.

10th April	15th April	19th April
11mm	8mm	3mm

What is the difference between the rainfall on 10th April and 19th April?

☐ mm

1 mark

On the 30th April there was 11mm more rain fall than 19th April

What was the amount of rainfall on 30th April?

☐ mm

1 mark

3 A clock shows the time Joan left her home.

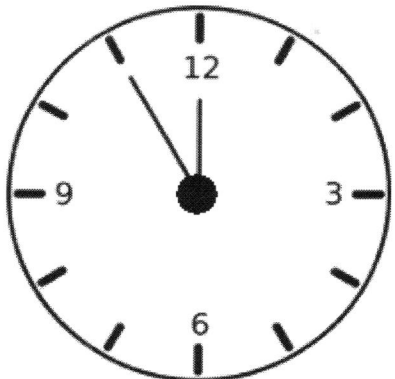

She walked to work for 25 minutes.

What time did she reach work?

| : |

1 mark

She left work 7 hours and 45 minutes later.

At what time did she leave work?

| : |

1 mark

4 Each shape stands for a number

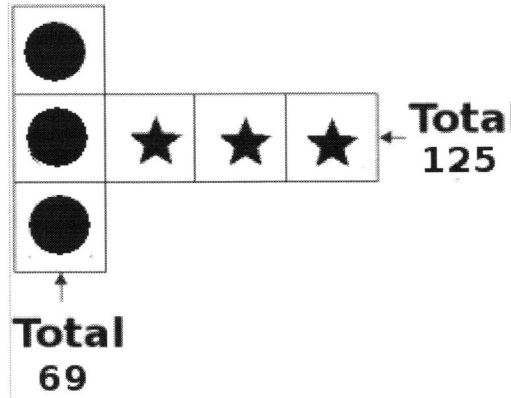

Work out the **value** of each shape.

● = [ ]   1 mark

★ = [ ]   1 mark

5 Write these fractions in order starting with the **smallest.**

1/4   3/4   1/2   5/6   1/3

[ ] [ ] [ ] [ ] [ ]
smallest

1 mark

6 Jo cuts a 450 cm ribbon in to **three** pieces.

The length of the first piece is **2.7** metres.

The length of the second piece is **1.73** metres.

What is the length of the third piece?

Show your method

cm

2 marks

7 Olive buys **four** pencils.

She pays with a £2 coin

This is her change.

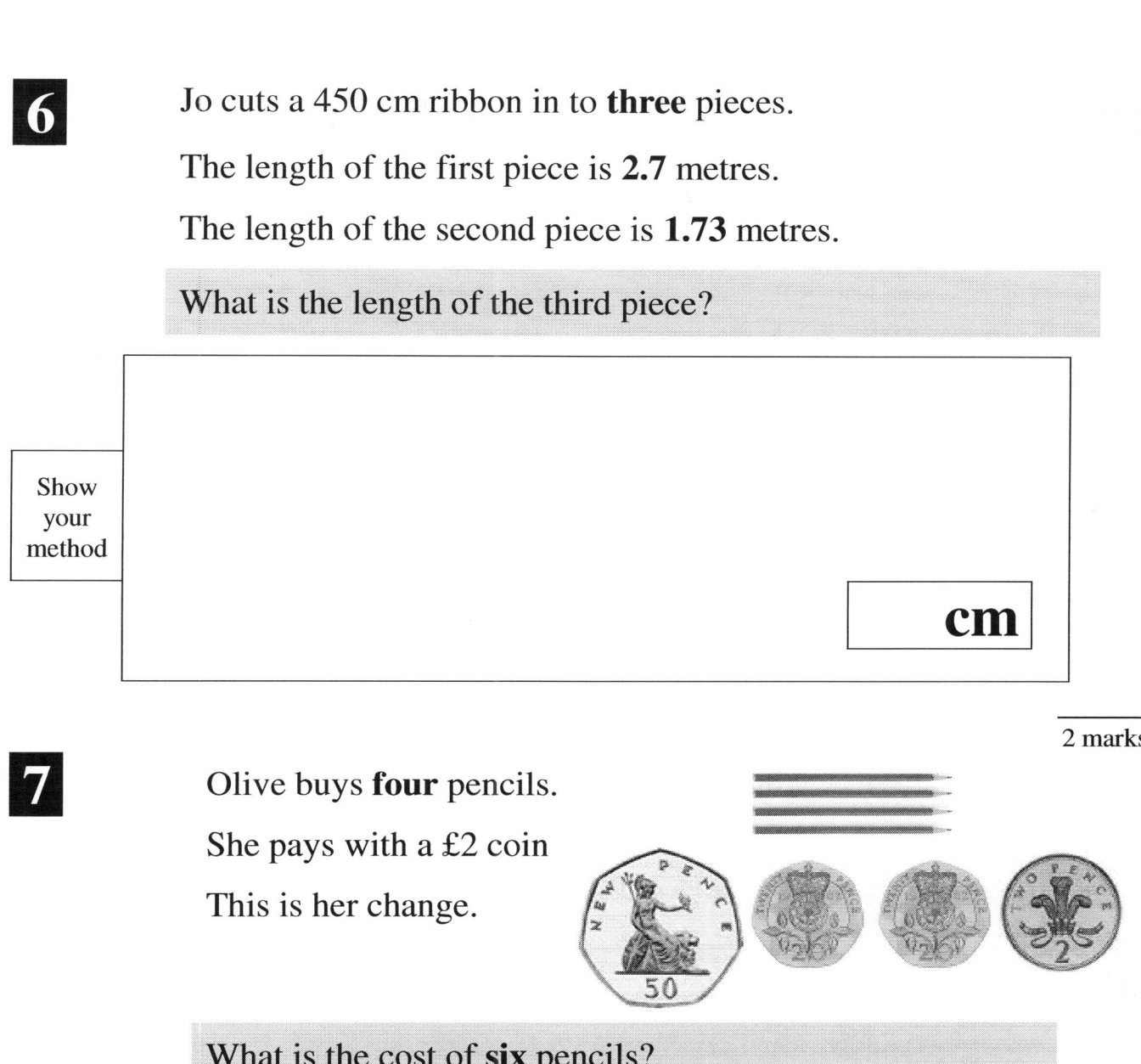

What is the cost of **six** pencils?

Show your method

£ .

2 marks

8 Here are five angles marked on a grid of squares.

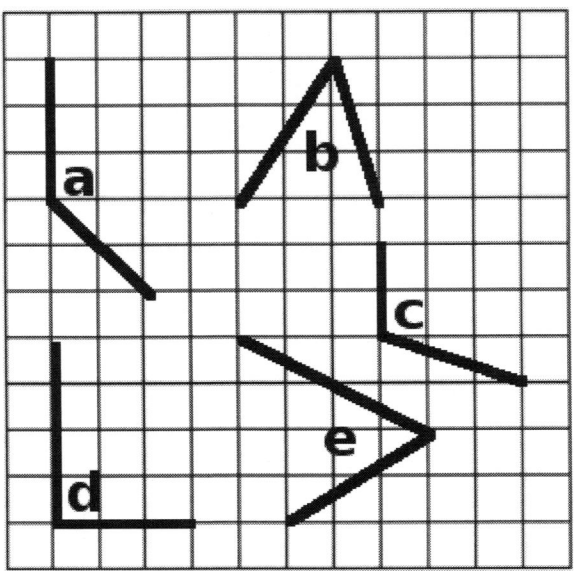

Write the letters of the angles that are **obtuse.**

_____ 1 mark

Write the letters of the angles that are **acute.**

_____ 1 mark

9 Here is part of a train timetable from Birmingham New Street to London Euston.

Birmingham New Street	8:01	8:17	8:21	8:47
Coventry	8:27	8:43	8:49	9:14
Milton Keynes Central	8:57	9:12	9:21	9:44
Watford Junction	9:17	9:32	9:41	10:06
London Euston	9:41	9:56	10:05	10:30

How many minutes does it take for the 8:17 from Birmingham New Street to reach Coventry?

[ ] minutes

1 mark

Mr Brown is at Milton Keynes Central at 9:15.

What is the earliest time he can reach Watford Junction?

[:]

1 mark

10 A single cube had a length of 1cm.

Elle used eight cubes to make a cuboid as below.

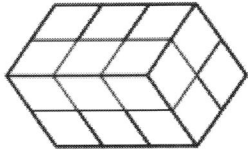

What is the volume of the cuboid?

cm³

1 mark

11 A shop orders 12 crates of fizzy pop.

Each crate contains 24 cans.

Each can contains 250 ml.

How many litres of fizzy pop were ordered?

Show your method

litres

2 marks

12 A triangle is translated from position **A** to **B**.

Complete the sentence.

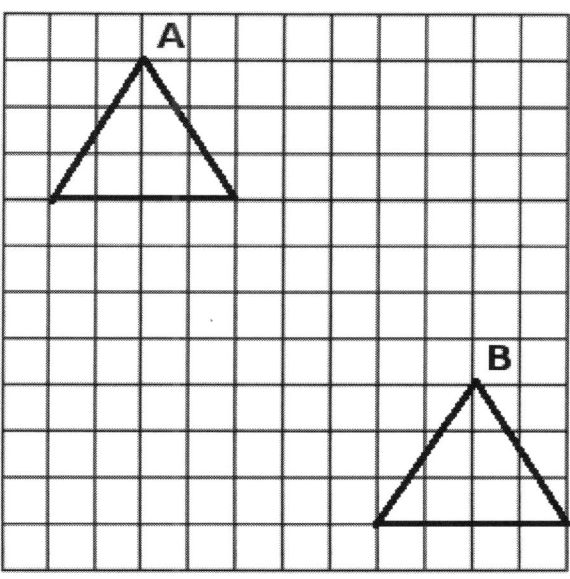

The triangle has moved ☐ squares down

and ☐ squares to the right.

1 mark

13 Lisa chooses a number.

She divides it by 7 and then subtracts 7.

She multiplies this result by 7.

Her answer is 28

What was the number she started with?

Show your method

2 marks

14 Complete each sentence using a number **from the list below.**

24   60   1,440   10,080   604,800

There are [   ] minutes in a day.

1 mark

There are [   ] seconds in a week.

1 mark

15 Complete this table by rounding the numbers to the **nearest integer.**

	Rounded to the **nearest integer**
235.4	
963.5	
8139.9	

2 marks

16 6 stars have the same mass 9 circles.

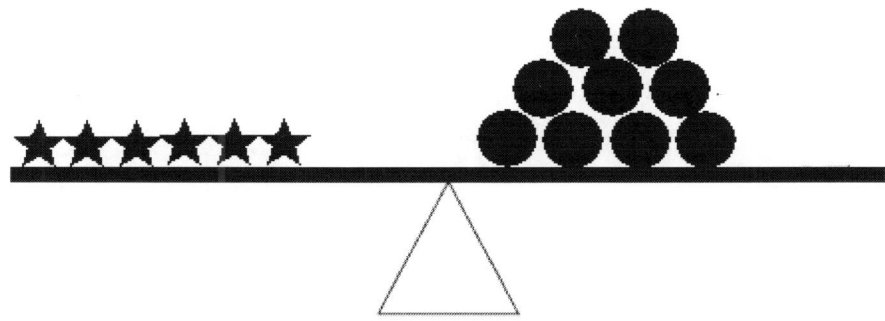

The mass of a circle is 5g.

What is the mass of a star?

Show your method

____ g

2 marks

17 Here is an isosceles triangle.

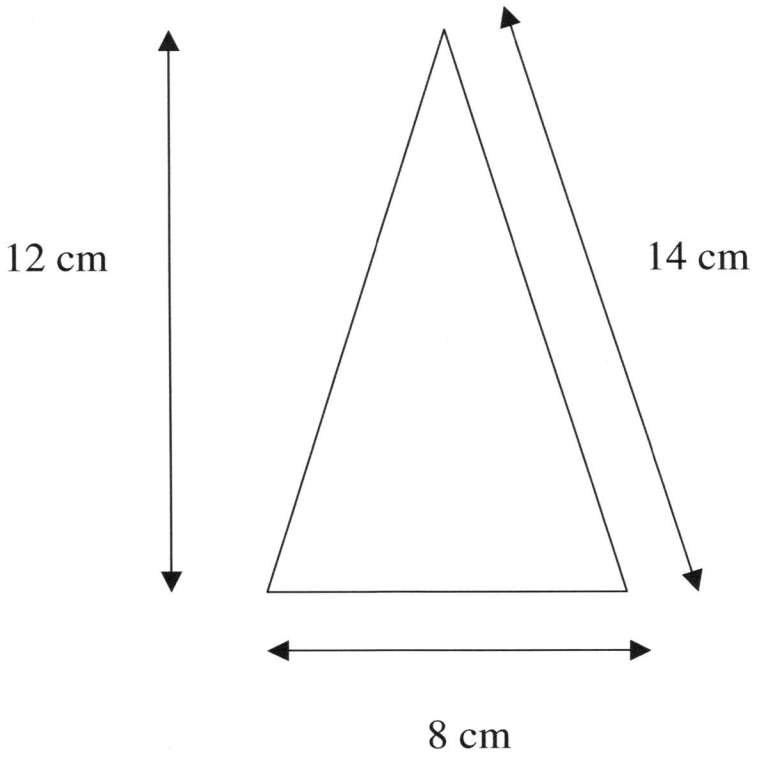

What is the area of the triangle?

☐ cm²

1 mark

18 Here are four quadrilaterals.

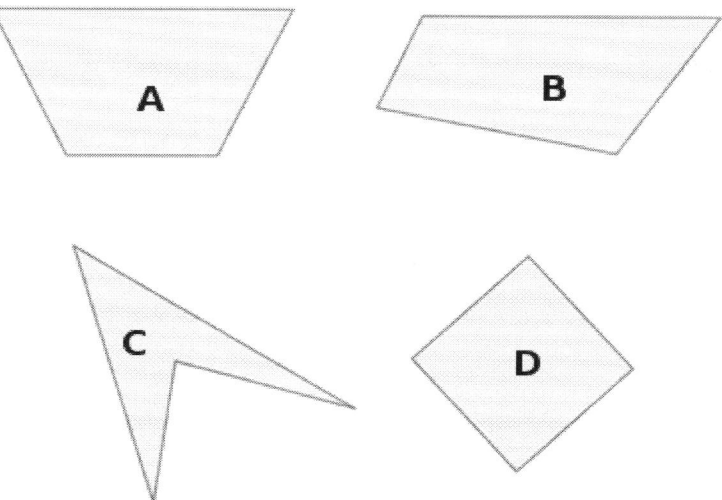

Enter the letter of the quadrilateral that has **no** acute or obtuse angles.

1 mark

Enter the letter of the quadrilateral that has **three** acute angles.

1 mark

19 Circle the two numbers that multiply to equal 1 million.

2   500   2,000   100,000   5,000,000

1 mark

20

Linda had some money.

She spent £2.75 on some cereal bars.

She purchased three apples at 25p each.

She spent one-quarter of her money.

How much money did Lisa have to start with?

Show your method

£   .

2 marks

The test is now over. If you have time, check your answers.

National curriculum mock test
Key stage 2

Mathematics

Paper 3: Reasoning

You have 40 minutes to complete this test which contains 20 questions, with 35 marks available.

First name	
Middle name	
Last name	
Date of birth	**Day** **Month** **Year**
School name	

MOCK TEST E

1 Write the missing numbers.

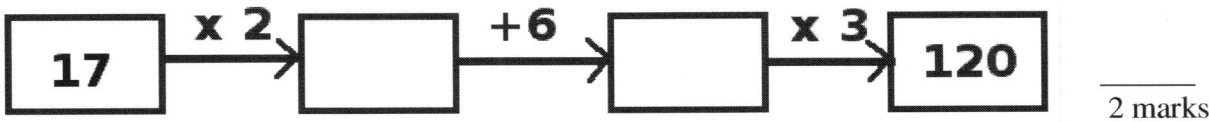

2 marks

2 This table shows the average temperature on certain days during December.

8th Dec	15th Dec	19th Dec	22nd Dec
-1 °C	3 °C	-5 °C	-2 °C

The average temperature on 15th December was twice that of 10th December.

What was the average temperature on 10th December?

1 mark

On the 21st December the temperature was 7 degrees lower than on 19th December.

What was the average temperature on 21st December?

1 mark

3 This graph shows the temperature in various cities.

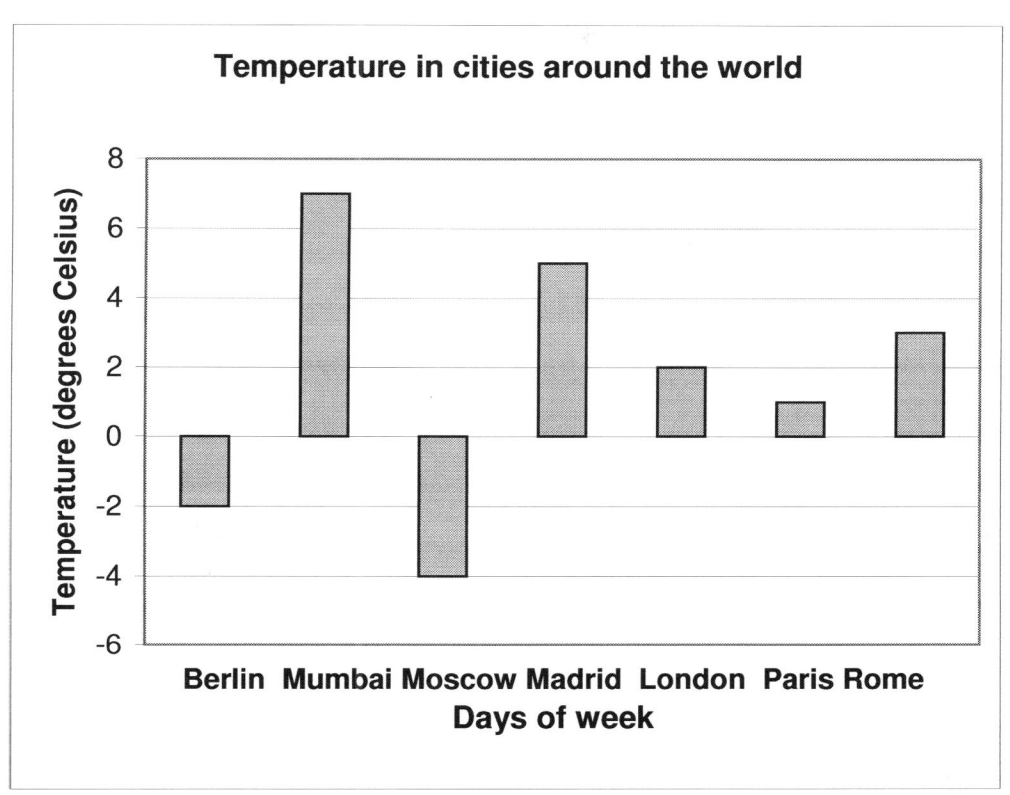

What is the range of the temperature?

☐ °C

1 mark

What is the median temperature?

☐ °C

1 mark

4 Here are some shapes made of rectangles.

Shade the rectangles so one quarter of each shape is shaded.

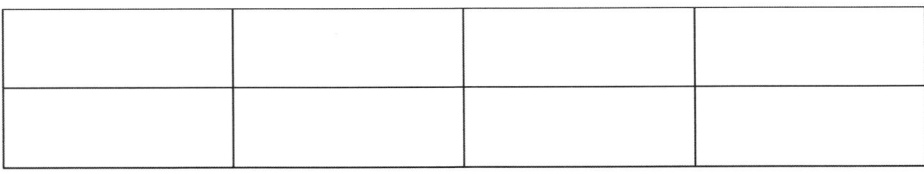

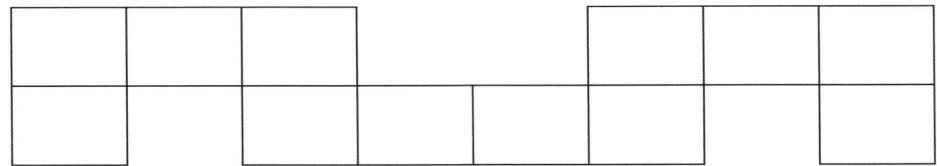

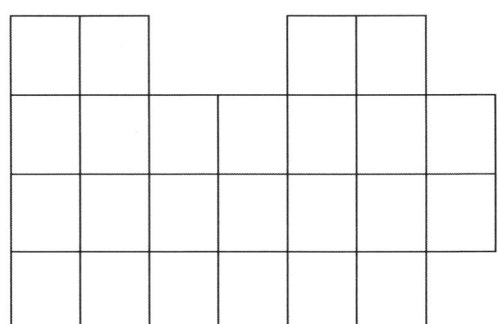

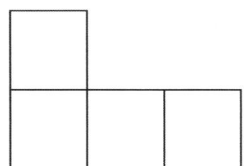

2 marks

5 Write these numbers in order starting with the **smallest.**

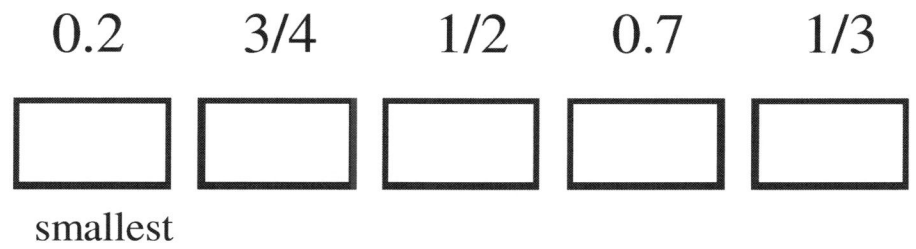

0.2   3/4   1/2   0.7   1/3

smallest

1 mark

6 Sam had a piece of string that he cut in to three pieces.

The length of the first piece was 3.2 metres.

The length of the second piece was 1.5 times as large as the second piece.

The third piece was twice as large as the second piece.

What is the length of the piece of Sam's string?

Show your method

. m

2 marks

65

7

A pack of **four** pencils of £1.25.

A pack of 3 pencils costs £0.90.

The three packs were on special offer: buy two get the third at half price.

Harry wanted to buy 12 pencils in total.

How much would Harry save by purchasing the three packs on special offer?

Show your method

£ .

2 marks

8

Amy rolls two dice.

What is the probability the total of the dice will be 12?

Show your method

2 marks

9 Here is a shaded shape on a grid.

The shape is translated so that point A moves to point B.

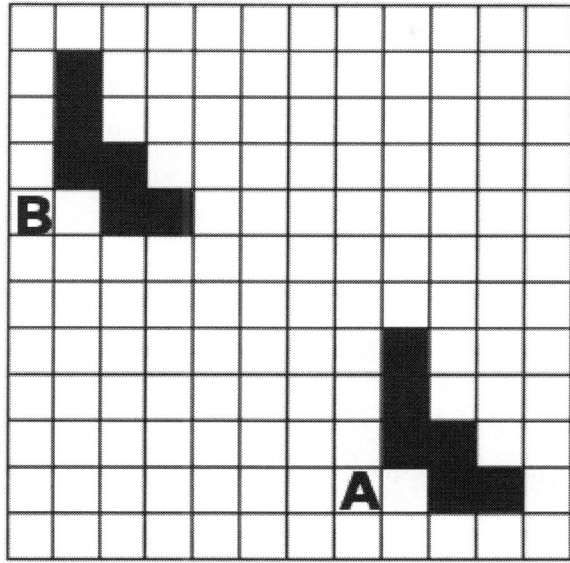

The shape has moved ☐ squares up

and ☐ squares to the left.

1 mark

10 Anne leaves home at 8:15 and walks to the bus stop.

She catches the 8:23 bus to work, which arrives at 8:41.

She then arrives at work 10 minutes later.

How many minutes was the bus journey?

| mins |

1 mark

How long was Anne's total journey time from home to work?

| mins |

1 mark

11 A single cube is 2cm wide.

Elle used twelve cubes to make the cuboid as shown.

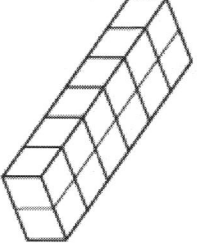

What is the volume of the cuboid?

| cm³ |

1 mark

12 Amy buys a jumper in the sale.

The price tag was £12.50.

There was a 30% discount off the price tag.

How much did Amy pay for the jumper?

Show your method

£   .

2 marks

13 Circle the two numbers that add to equal 1 million.

600,000   40,000   249,999   60,000   750,001

1 mark

14 Amy and Elle have 30 marbles between them.

Amy has 8 marbles more than Elle.

How many marbles does Amy have?

Show your method

2 marks

15 Complete each sentence.

There are ☐ prime numbers between 4 and 20.

1 mark

There are ☐ square numbers between 3 and 50.

1 mark

16 Complete this table by rounding the sums to the **nearest integer.**

	Rounded to the **nearest integer**
12.5 + 9.7	
12.1 − 13.3	
12.9 − 7.5	

2 marks

17 Elle drew a shape of a quadrilateral.

All the sides were of equal length.

All the angles were either acute or obtuse.

Select the best description of the shape Elle drew.

Rectangle ☐   Square ☐

Parallelogram ☐   Rhombus ☐

1 mark

18 This clock shows the time as 4 o'clock.

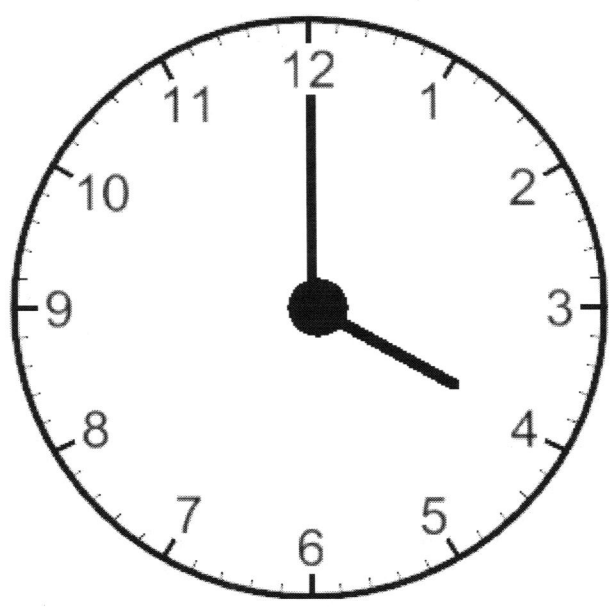

What is the acute angle between the clock hands?

Show your method

°

2 marks

19 A garden measures 17 m x 9 m.

It consists of lawn that measures 15m x 7m surrounded by a path.

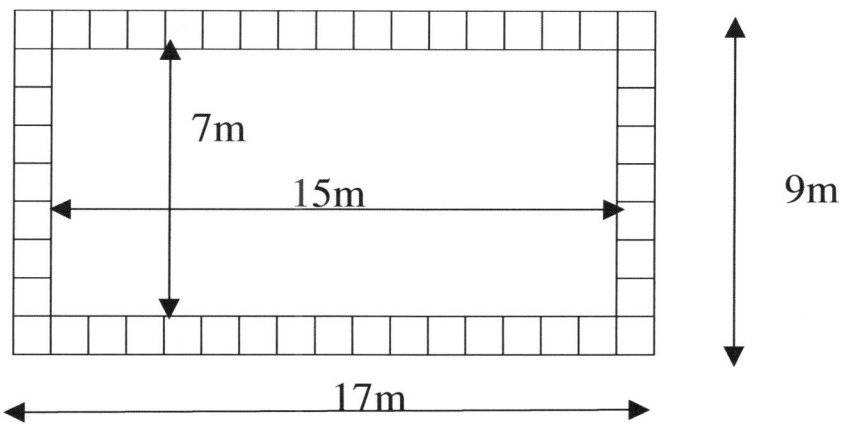

What is the total area of the path.

Show your method

m²

2 marks

20 Amy saw an advert for a new computer online.

The price of the computer was £480 after a 20% discount.

What was the price of the computer before the discount?

Show your method

£

2 marks

The test is now over. If you have time, check your answers.

Test A Answers (35 marks)

Q	Answer	Explanation
1	One of:	Numerous answers.
A	36, 72…	Use multiplication tables
B	9, 18, 27…	to check multiples
C	1, 2, 3, 5…	2 correct: 1 mark
		3 correct: 2 marks
2A	-15 1 mark	$-7 - 8 = -15$
B	1 1 mark	$-7 + 8 = 1$
3A	7 1 mark	HTU.th
B	9 1 mark	327**8**5.7**9**
4A	July	June = 50. July = 90
	September	Aug = 40. Sep = 70 1m
B	£130	90 + 40 = 130 1 mark
5	(scale showing 50 to 100) 1 mark	150ml – 65ml = 85ml. Between 50 and 100 are 5 sections. Each section is 50/5 = 10ml. 65 is halfway from 60 & 70.
6A	÷ 100	7.6 ÷ 100 = 0.076
B	x 1000	7.6 x 1000 = 7600
C	÷ 10	7.6 ÷ 10 = 0.76
		2 correct: 1 mark
		3 correct: 2 marks
7	Sixty seven thousand, nine hundred and eighty three.	Units = 3, Tens = 8, Hundreds = 9, Thousands = 7, Ten thousands = 6 1 mark
8	(grid with kite A moved to B)	A moved 3 squares down and 6 squares to the right. Count squares 3 down and 6 squares to the right each corner.
	2m correct. 1 mark if out by 1 square	
9	32.4g	7.2/2 = 3.6 1 mark
		3 x 7.2 = 21.6 working
		3 x 3.6 = 10.8 + 2 marks
		32.4 correct
10	5p	Sweets = 80/4p = 20p
	1m working	Choc = £1.50/6 = 25p
	1m correct	25p – 20p = 5p
11	11	2 + 5 = 7
	4942	4 + 6 = 10. 0 carry 1
	3365 +	1 + 9 + 3 = 13 carry 1
	8307	1 + 3 + 4 = 8
		1 mark 2 or 3 correct.
		2 marks if all 4 correct.
12	0.994	1 – 0.006 = 0.994
13	3: order	4/6 = 2/3 = 48/72
	7/18 <	5/8 = 45/72
	6/12 <	6/12 = 1/2 = 36/72
	5/8 <	7/18 = 28/72
	4/6 1 mark	7/18 < 6/12 < 5/8 < 4/6
14	(pyramid: 30 / 7.5, 4 / 3.75, 2, 2)	2 x ? = 4. ? = 4/2 = 2
	1m if 2 correct	? x 4 = 30 ? 30/4 = 7.5
	2 m, all	? x 2 = 7.5.
		? = 7.5/2 = 3.75
15	Many (trapezium shape)	1 mark
16	48	n ÷ 4 + 13 ÷ 2 = 12.5
		No BOMAS backwards
		12.5 x 2 –13 x 4 = 48
		1 mark working
		2 marks correct
17	65%	Shaded = 7.
		White = 20 -- 7 = 13
	1 mark	% white = 13/20 x 100%
		= 13 x 5 = 65%
18	180g	80: 60 sugar
		240: x spread
		spread 60/80 x 240
		= 180g 1 mark working
		2 marks if correct
19	133.28 m²	3
	1 mark for	4
	62.72 m²	9.8
	1 mark for	6.4 x
	subtraction	5880
	working	392
	3 marks	62.72
	if correct	196 – 62.72 = 133.28
20A	(0,7) 1m	Triangle height = 9-7 = 2
		A = (0, [9 - 2]) = (0,7)
B	(8,2) 1m	B = (8, [0 + 2]) = (8,2)

Test B Answers (35 marks)

Q	Answer	Explanation
1A	62	78 − 16 = 62
B	110	94 + 16 = 110
C	158	142 + 16 = 158
		2 correct: 1 mark
		3 correct: 2 marks
2A	12 °C 1m	7 − =5 = 7 + 5 = 12 °C
B	−3 °C 1m	2 − 5 = −3 °C
3	4:15, 16:15	4:15 = (4+12):15 = 16:15
		1 mark
4A	23 1 mark	4 stars = 92
		1 star = 92/4 = 23
B	17 1 mark	2 circles + 23 = 57
		2 circles=34 1 circle=17
5	0.069, 0.503, 0.68, 5.001, 6.7 1 mark	
6	41	2 + 1.27 + 1.32 = 4.59
		5 − 4.57 = 0.41m = 41cm
		1 mark working
		2 for correct answer.
7A	a,b,d 1m	Acute angles are less
B	c,e 1 m	than 90° and obtuse more than 90°
8	27p	50p+20p+20p+2p =92p
		£2 − 92p = 108p
		108p/4 = 27p
		1 mark working out
		2 marks if correct.
9A	17 1 mark	9:13 − 8:56 =13 + 4 = 17 mins
B	8:59 1 mark	Next train after 7:55 is 8:32 arrives at 8:59.
10	E 1 mark	A=6x2=12 B=3x2=12
		C=12x1=12 D=6x2=12
		E=3x3=9
11	2688	12 x 8 = 96
		96 x 28 = 2688
		(2800 − 4 x 28 = 2688)
		1 mark working out.
		2 marks correct answer
12	6	Count 7 up and
	7	7 to the left 1 mark
13	42	$n \div 3 − 7 \times 4 = 28$ reverse
		$28 \div 4 + 7 \times 3 = 42$
		1 mark working out.
		2 marks correct answer
14A	168 1m	24 x 7 = 168
B	10,080 1m	168 x 60 = 10,080
15A	30,600	Look at tens. If 4 or less
B	3,100	keep hundreds digit same
C	300	else increase by 1.
		2 correct: 1 mark
		3 correct: 2 marks
16	2.5g	6 stars = 3.5 x 6 = 21g
		7 circles = 21g
		1 circle = 21/7 = 3g
		1 mark working out.
		2 marks correct answer
17	C 1 mark	A = 4 x 2 /2 = 4
		B = 4 x 2 /2 = 4
		C = 3 x 3 /2 = 4.5
		D = 4 x 2 /2 = 4
		E = 2 x 4/2 = 4
18	Rhombus (2nd shape)	Diagonals of a rhombus cross at right angles. 1m
19	250 & 4000 1m	1 million − 1,000,000
		250 x 400 = 1,000,000
20	£3.00	£1.50 + £0.75 = £2.25
		£2.25 = ¾ as ¼ left
		£2.25 x 4/3 = 1 (all)
		=9/3 = £3
		1 mark working out.
		2 marks correct answer
21	5706	19 x 317 = 6023 1 mark
		18 x 317 = 6023 − 317
		= 5076
		1 mark working out.
		2 marks correct answer as long as correct working.

Test C Answers (35 marks)

Q	Answer	Explanation
1A B C	21, 42… 7,14,28.. 1,2,4,..	Many answers. Use tables 2 correct: 1 mark 3 correct: 2 marks
2A B	77 1m 7 1m	7 x 11 = 77 (tables) ? x 12 = 84. ? = 84/12 = 7
3A B	1 1m 3 1m	tHTU.th 61427.31
4A B	May, July, August £210	April = 120 May = 60 June = 90 July = 60 Aug=60 1 mark £120 + £90 = £210 1 mark
5	70ml	135ml – 65ml = 70ml 1 mark
6A B C	x100 ÷ 1000 ÷ 10	1.01 x 100 = 101 10.01 ÷ 1000 = 0.01001 0.101 ÷ 10 = 0.0101 2 correct = 1 mark 3 correct = 2 marks
7	Sixty-six thousand seven hundred and twenty four	tT,HTU 66,724 724 = seven hundred and twenty four 66 = sixty six thousand 1 mark
8A	As shown 6 to the left and 4 up.	2 marks correct. 1 mark if one square out
9A	30g	5p = 3g, so 10p = 2x3g = 6g (6x4) + (2x3) = 24 + 6 = 30g 1 marks correct answer. 1 mark correct method
10	£0.35	2 balls + book = £1.75 4 balls+2 books=£1.75x2=£3.5 2 books = £3.50 - £2.80=£0.70 1 book = £0.70/2 = £0.35 1 mark working 1 mark for answer

Q	Answer	Explanation
11	9701 - 2586 7115	Units 11 – ? = 10, so ? = 6 (? – 1) – 8 = 1. so ? = 10 so digit = 0 (7 – 1) = ? = 1, so ? = 5 ? – 2 = 7, so ? = 9 2 or 3 correct, 1 mark 3 correct, 2 marks
12	0.957	1 – 0.043 = 0/957
13	3 in the order	0.51 > 0.50 > 0.47 > 0.4 1 mark
14	140 / 14 10 / 3.5 4 2.5	210/4 = 2.5 140/10 = 14 14/4 = 3/5 3 correct: 2 marks 2 correct: 1 mark
15	Many options Eg as shown	1 mark
16	66	n ÷ 3 + 12 ÷4 = 8.5 Reverse, no BODMAS 8.5 x 4 – 12 x 3 = 66 1 mark working 1 mark for answer
17	15% 1m	3/20 = 15/100 = 15%
18	20g	Whole milk 125/25 = 5 Caster sugar = 100/5 =20g 1 mark working 1 mark for answer
19	80 m^2	18 x 9 = 18 x 10 – 18 = 180 – 18 = 162 1 mark 162 – 82 = 80 1 mark
20	79 1 m	78 x79 = 6162 6162/79 = 78. 78+1 = 79
21A B	(6, 7) 1m (-6,2) 1m	Triangle width = 6 Triangle height = 9-7 = 2 A = (0 + 6, 7) = (6,7) B = (-6, 0 + 2) = (-6,2) 1 mark each

Test D Answers (35 marks)

Q	Answer	Explanation
1A	50	88 − 18 = 50
B	104	86 + 18 = 104
C	122	104 + 18 = 122
		1 mark: 1 or 2 correct
		2 marks: 3 correct
2A	8 mm	11 − 3 = 8 1 mark
B	14mm	3 + 11 = 14 1 mark
3A	12:20	Clock: 11:55 add 25=12:20 1m
B	20:05	12:20 + 7:45 = 20:05 1m
4A	23 1m	3 circles = 69,
		1 circle = 69/3 = 23
B	34 1m	23 + 3 stars = 125
		3 stars = 102
		1 star = 102/3 = 34
5	1/4, 1/3, 1/2, 3/4, 5/6 1m	1/4 = 3/12 3/4 = 9/12 1/2 = 6/12 5/6 = 1s/12 1/3 = 4/12 3/12< 4/12< 6/12< 9/12< 10/12 1/4 < 1/3 < ½ < 3/4 < 5/6
6	7 cm	4500cm = 4.5 m 2.7 + 1.73 = 4.43 1 mark 4.50 − 4.43 =0 .07m = 7cm 1 mark
7A	£1.62	50 + 20 + 20 + 2 = 92p £2 − 92p = 108p 108/4 = 27p = £0.27 1 mark £0.27 x 6 = £1.62 1 mark
8A	a, c 1m	Obtuse > 90° = a and c
B	b, e 1m	Acute < 90° = b and e
		d = right angle = 90°
9A	26 1m	8:43 - 8:17 = 26 mins
B	9:41 1m	Next train is 9:21 reaches 9:41
10	12 1m	l x w x h = 3 x 2 x 2 = 12 cm^3
11	72	12 x 24 = 12 x 12 x 2 144 x 2 = 288 1 mark 250ml = ¼ litre 288/4 = 72 litres 1 mark
12	6 & 7	A to B: 6 to the right and 7 down. 1 mark

Q	Answer	Explanation
13	77	n ÷7 − 7 x 7 = 28 Reverse, no BODMAS 28 ÷ 7 + 7 x 7 = 77 1 mark working 1 mark correct answer
14A	1,440	24 hours x 60 mins = 1440 1 mark
B	604,800	1 week: 1440 x 7 = 10,080 10,080 x 60 = 604,800 1 mark
15A	235	If 4 or less round down
B	964	If 5 or above round up
C	8140	39.9 becomes 40
		2 correct 1: mark
		3 correct: 2 marks
16	7.5g	Circles: 9 x 5 = 45g 6 stars 45g 1 star = 45/6 = 7.5g Correct answer: 1 mark Working out: 1 mark

17	48 cm^2	Area = base x height/2
		       = 8 x 12/2
		       = 48 cm^2 1 mark

18A	D 1m	Acute is < 90° Obtuse > 90° D is a square, all 90°
B	C 1m	C has 3 acute angles
19	500 2,000	1 million = 1,000,000 500 x 2,000 = 1000,000 1 mark
20	£14.00	3 x 25p = 75p = £0.75 £2.75 + £0.75 = £3.50 £.3.50 = ¼, so £3.50 x 4 = £14.00 which is all of it. 1 mark working 1 mark correct answer

Test E Answers (35 marks)

Q	Answer	Explanation
1A	34 1m	17 x 2 = 34
	40 1m	34 + 6 = 40
2A	1.5 °C 1m	3/2 = 1.5
B	-12 °C 1m	-5 –7 = -12
3A	11 °C 1m	7 - -4 = 7 + 4 = 11
B	2 °C 1m	7 days 4th one in order = 2
4	Shade any	
A	2	8: ¼ = 2
B	3	12: ¼ = 3
C	6	24: ¼ = 6
D	1	4: ¼ = 1
		2 marks: all correct
		1 mark: 2 or 3 correct
5	0.2	¾ = 0/75.
	1/3	½ = 0.5
	1/2	1/3 = 0.333
	0.7	
	3/4	1 mark
6	17.6m	1st = 3.2
		2nd = 3.2 x 1.5 = 4.8
		3rd = 4.8 x 2 = 9.6
		3.2 + 4.8 + 9.6 = 17.6
		1 mark working
		1 mark correct answer
7	£0.60	4 pencils = £1.25.
		12 = £1.25 x 3 = £3.75
		3 pack: £0.90 x 3 + £0.45 = £3.15
		Savings=£3.75-£3.15 =£0.60
		1 mark working
		1 mark correct answer
8	1/36	12 means roll 6 twice = 1/6 x 1/6 = 1/36
		1 mark working out
		1 mark correct answer
9	6 up	Count squares up and left
	7 left	1 mark if both correct
10A	18 min 1m	8:41 – 8:23 = 18 mins
B	36 min 1m	8:41 + 10 = 8:51
		8:51 – 8:15 = 36 mins
11	96 cm^3 1m	2 x 4 x 12 = 96 cm^3
12	£8.75	£12.50 x 10% = £1.25
		30% = £1.25 x 3 = £3.75
		£12.50 - £3.75 = £8.75
		1 mark working out
		1 mark correct answer
13	249,999	1 million = 1,000,000
	750,001	249,999
		750,001 -
	1 mark	1000,000
14	19	30 – 8 = 22
		22 ÷ 2 = 11
		11+ 8 = 19 marbles
		1 mark working
		1 mark correct answer
15A	6 1m	5,7,11,13,17,19
B	6 1m	4, 9, 16, 25, 36, 49
16A	22	12.5 + 9.7 = 22.2 → 22
B	-1	12.1 – 13.3 = -1.2 → -1
C	5	12.9 – 7.5 = 5.4 → 5
		1 mark: 2 correct
		2 marks: 3 correct
17	Rhombus	Quadrilateral: 4 sides
		Equal sizes: square or
	1 mark	rhombus
		angles acute or obtuse – rhombus
18	120°	Circle = 360°
		360/12 = 30°
		Acute is between 12 and 4
		= 4 x 30° = 120°
		1 mark for working out
		1 mark for correct answer
19	48 m^2	17 x 9 = 153
		15 x 7 = 105 - 1 mark
		84 1 mark
20	£600	£850 = 80%
		£480 = 1%
		80
		£480 x 100 = 100%
		80
		= £600
		1 mark: working out
		1 mark: correct answer

Converting key stage 2 raw scores to scaled scores for 2016 tests

The tables show each of the possible raw scores on the 2016 key stage 2 mathematics tests.

To convert each pupil's raw score to a scaled score, look up the raw score and read across to the appropriate scaled score.

A scaled score of 100 or more shows the pupil has met the expected standard in the test.

Pupils need to have a raw score of 3 marks to be awarded the minimum scaled score.

If a pupil has a raw score of 0 to 2 marks, the scaled score field on return of results will be left blank.

Mathematics		Mathematics		Mathematics		Mathematics		Mathematics	
Raw Score	Scaled Score	Raw Score	Scaled Score	Raw Score	Scaled Score	Raw Score	Scaled Score	Raw Score	Scaled Score
0	No Scaled Score (N)	23	89	45	96	67	101	89	106
1		24	90	46	96	68	101	90	107
2		25	90	47	97	69	101	91	107
3	80	26	90	48	97	70	102	92	107
4	80	27	91	49	97	71	102	93	108
5	80	28	91	50	97	72	102	94	108
6	80	29	91	51	98	73	102	95	109
7	80	30	92	52	98	74	103	96	109
8	81	31	92	53	98	75	103	97	109
9	82	32	92	54	98	76	103	98	110
10	82	33	93	55	98	77	103	99	110
11	83	34	93	56	99	78	104	100	111
12	84	35	93	57	99	79	104	101	111
13	84	36	94	58	99	80	104	102	112
14	85	37	94	59	99	81	104	103	113
15	86	38	94	60	100	82	105	104	113
16	86	39	94	61	100	83	105	105	114
17	87	40	95	62	100	84	105	106	115
18	87	41	95	63	100	85	105	107	116
19	88	42	95	64	100	86	106	108	117
20	88	43	96	65	101	87	106	109	119
21	88	44	96	66	101	88	106	110	120
22	89								

CoolCleverKids

"...because it's COOL to be CLEVER"

Come on, you do the maths!

11+ & KS1, KS2 Maths, NVR, Science, Spellings

Maths Programme only	CoolCleverKids ™	Kumon ™
Cost Per Month	From £20/month	From £55/month
Lesson Notes	Yes	No
Video Lesson Links	Yes	No
Online Worksheets	Yes	No
Automatic Marking	Yes	No
KS1 & KS2 SATs Based Tests	Yes	No
Automatic Revision Tests	Yes	No
Categorised Reports	Yes	No
Performance Graphs	Yes	No
Links to Numerous Games	Yes	No
Unlimited Access	Yes	No
KS2 SATs Spelling Tests	Yes	No
KS2 SATs Science Tests	Yes	No
11+ Non verbal reasoning (NVR)	Yes	No
No Wasted Travel Time or Cost	Yes	No

All trade marks acknowledged & prices correct at time of comparison. Kumon is often £60+ per month.

Printed in Great Britain
by Amazon